To an Unknown Goddess

To an Unknown Goddess

Poems and Literary Fragments

TIMOTHY P. JACKSON

RESOURCE *Publications* • Eugene, Oregon

TO AN UNKNOWN GODDESS
Poems and Literary Fragments

Copyright © 2024 Timothy P. Jackson. All rights reserved. Except for brief quotations in critical publications or reviews, no part of this book may be reproduced in any manner without prior written permission from the publisher. Write: Permissions, Wipf and Stock Publishers, 199 W. 8th Ave., Suite 3, Eugene, OR 97401.

Resource Publications
An Imprint of Wipf and Stock Publishers
199 W. 8th Ave., Suite 3
Eugene, OR 97401

www.wipfandstock.com

PAPERBACK ISBN: 978-1-6667-3434-8
HARDCOVER ISBN: 978-1-6667-9009-2
EBOOK ISBN: 978-1-6667-9010-8
VERSION NUMBER 11/08/24

*You, my heart's sovereign mistress . . .,
stored in the deepest recesses of my heart,
in my most brimmingly vital thoughts,
there where it is equally far to heaven as to hell
—unknown divinity!*

—Søren Kierkegaard

Contents

To an Unknown Goddess | 1

I. *Eros* and Justice

Thorn in the Flesh | 5
Hylas's Folly | 7
To a Scholar on Her Birthday | 8
Waiting | 9
Love's Hands | 10
Love Lost | 11
Well, Donne? | 12
Gifts of Dust | 13
Anorexia | 14
Reasons to Burn | 15
Paschal Hearts | 16
Buster in the Big City | 18
Adam's Elation or the Gynecological Argument
    for the Existence of God | 20
Erotic Voices | 21
Fallen | 22
Jeffrey Dahmer, RIP | 24
Ifs | 25
Flesh in the Thorn | 26
Word and Flesh | 27
Broken Haiku | 28
Too Deep for Words | 29
Does Death? | 30
Multiverses | 31

The Truth Cult | 32
Indefinite Article | 33
Memorial Day: In Honor of George Floyd | 35
Short Stuff: A Tale of Redemption | 36
Second Timothy | 40

II. *Philia* and Humor

Haiku for Wendell Berry | 45
An Era's Warmest Eye | 46
Orlando Furioso 2 | 47
Bloomsday | 49
The Genius of Key West | 50
For John Keats | 52
Just a Smile at Auden | 54
Without Enemy or Immortality? | 56
The Art of Poetry | 57
The Found Poet: James Tate, RIP | 58
Song for Gail | 59
Who Will Wait With Poetry? | 60
Counting | 62
Cyrus's Children | 63
Whittaker Chambers, RIP | 64
Kentucky Paradoxes | 65
Icons in Old Louisville | 67
The Pacific | 68
Blowing Our Qi | 69
Sending Regrets | 70
Loving Anne Sexton | 71
Was Heist Martin Heidegger | 73
Some English Language Writers | 74
Haiku for Autumnal Yale | 75
A Tourist Pets the Sphinx | 76
Catechism | 77
Anti-Heroes | 78
Ancient Graffiti | 80
The End of the Oral Tradition | 81

A Brief History of Science | 82
A Liberal History of Western Thought | 83
Rules for Saint George Renters | 84
A Jewish Joyce Kilmer | 86
To Florence to See the Moon | 87
The Avuncular Visitor | 88
Eternal Life | 90
In Sickness and in Health | 91
Despair | 92
The Birth of the Lamb | 93

III. *Agape* and Forgiveness

One Surpassing Poem | 97
My Prayer of Sainte Simone | 99
Petition | 101
Holiness | 102
Eastern Orthdoxy | 103
To the Eternal Mother | 104
Divine Fertility | 105
Insufficient Unto Yesterday Is the Good Thereof | 107
Matters of Life and Death | 109
The Earwig | 112
Simple Gifts | 113
All Saints Day: A Gothic Romance | 114
The Immaculate Conception Conceived | 115
The Love of God | 116
Inward and Outward | 118
The Amniotic Sack | 119
Bernini's Saint Teresa | 121
Saint Catherine's Silk Bag | 123
A Friday Dialogue | 124
Sonnet of a Philo-Semite | 126
A Prayer to and for the Jewish People, After Auschwitz | 127
Pogrom's Progress: A Christmas Poem 2023 | 129
The Descent of Goodness | 130
Making Sense of Christ | 132

Caste and Christ | 133
Eternal Returns (12–25-2019) | 134
One Small Step for Man | 135
Staring It Down | 137
Death's Carols | 138
Peace by the Book | 140
A Modern Ode | 141
Largillière's "Elizabeth Throckmorton" | 142
For Saint Elizabeth of Russia | 144
"Following Steadfast Love" | 146
Is There None Good? | 152
Divine Trifecta | 154
Coda: Unruly Disciplines | 155
Lux et Veritas? | 156
The Auschwitz Cross | 158
Sharing the Cross | 159
For Blessed Bernhard Lichtenberg, Righteous Among the Nations | 160
Reconnoitering Femininity | 162
June 24, 2022: The Healing Diet of Worms | 164
God Alone | 165
Apologies to Plato | 167
Scaling Man | 168
The Original Sin 2 | 170
Channeling Catherine | 171
The Gut of Rome | 172
Incarnation | 173
Transubstantiation | 174
In Adam's Place (After Reading Catherine of Siena) | 175
The Third Excellence (After Reading John of the Cross) | 176
Against Personolatry: My Poem of Saint Sandra Sabattini | 177
For Saints Weil and Hillesum | 179

Finale | 181

TO AN UNKNOWN GODDESS

Who was I
when she was my heart
and sun lifted sky
with a pulsing heat?

What was I
as she turned my head
and angels would sigh
over what I had?

When was I
while she was present
and time could cry
yet not resent?

Where am I
if each cosmic facet
expands like pi
from the beloved face?

Why am I
since she is ideal
Theia's bright eye
Plato's one idea?

How am I
to honor her grace

human but holy
above my race?

Her memory like cloves,
the bouquet of infinity,
inspires the three loves
for her unknown divinity.

I

Eros and Justice

THORN IN THE FLESH

Has any strong poet never wanted out,
Not when winter is on the heath
Or words rot like my Irish teeth,
But when the mind is free of doubt
And all within is all without,
Nothing above, nothing beneath,
White lilies on an evergreen wreath
Dreading not flood or drought?
For it cannot be repeated,
This monument sublime,
And the heart will be defeated
That tries to make it rhyme:
Beauty can be greeted
Only one time.

Has every erotic lover always wanted in,
Not in spite of fetid breath
Or the shame of flesh's death,
But when Venus without sin
Wears her soul upon her skin,
Redeeming Eve, Lady Macbeth,
Replacing Abel with wiser Seth,
Like high tide returns the ocean?
For it cannot be escheated,
This monument sublime,
And the heart will be defeated
That tries to make a dime:

Beauty can be deleted
For all time.

HYLAS'S FOLLY

With armored mind and heart unspoken
A joyful covenant signed, is broken
By the ancient fear of Hylas' folly
And goodness in a woman.

To this contorted pan of Janus,
Drunken bibber from the sacred chalice,
A pious lover pledges herself
And her sober trust.

Now, any eve may come a Circe
To Argonaut or quick Ulysses
And close the gym of his will
Training for high seas.

But to this world never-ending
The Muse of life is still descending
To write the pagan body and soul
Into the text of time.

So, acceptable siren, know the love
Of this former heir of Jove,
Receiving on the cresting waves
My self unlashed to any mast.

TO A SCHOLAR ON HER BIRTHDAY

Irrigate the earth with spittle from a kiss
And dry it with your raven hair;
Make the main an isle of bliss
By your simple presence there.

Filter from the sea the salt as from a tear
And touch it to your moistened lips;
Taste the savor in Trappist beer
And in your fingertips.

Resuscitate the sky with bouquet from a breath
And inebriate a winging dove;
But know you're a good and perfect gift
Given from above.

WAITING

> *But the faith and the love and the hope are all in the waiting.*
>
> —T.S. Eliot, "East Coker"

To describe the orbits of your blue eyes
Is not to praise you,
Yet I declare they are a sight
And mean a vision for my own.

To desire the warmth of your soft breasts
Is not to want you,
Yet I confess to the wanton desire
And more desirable wants than this.

To sense a tenderness in your twin heart
Is not to love you,
Yet I consider mine more fragile now
Than a shelled oyster in a cracked tumbler.

Devils are angels without the patience
To praise when wanting love,
So I wait in my empty office
For the coming of your smile.

LOVE'S HANDS

My love has hands you can live with
Her slender fingers butterfly antennae
Turning touch into light and time
Perfumed scent into sex and taste
First contact into lasting communion
Giving direction and balance
Holding without grasping
My heart.

LOVE LOST

As you let me go, dear One,
I swim up your tears to spawn
and wait before the fall is gone
for the hatching of our children.

Faith will be fair, as are you;
she'll love the light like a Jew
and know there is nothing new
to think or feel but to do.

Hope is a laughing infant
touched but for an instant
by a joy so contingent
it might almost be malignant.

Charity: who can ever say
why she'll come but never stay,
or how she'll live day to day
when death takes it all away?

The goddess tarries not for me;
my seed's adrift upon the sea;
I write these lines to set us free,
but there is no epiphany.

WELL, DONNE?

Lost love is a putrid meat
gathering flies for want of heat
once touching, vigorous tissue
now stunning fetor its sole issue.

Some baste eros' decay in rhyme
masking stench with words sublime
too late to freeze the rotting part
too late to cauterize the heart.

Others stutter through the pain
refusing to call a loss a gain
recalling once a bountiful meal
whimpering like a bashed harp seal

The best eat mute the poisoned scrap
taking the bait to reveal the trap
mouths open but tongues tied
recycling death in suicide.

GIFTS OF DUST

Love came away from burying love,
Dirt on its knees and under its nails,
Could not tell the living from the dead,
Not by odor or by crime;
Both were obedient to the clock,
Could be brushed off in no time,
Like homeless from a city block.

Hate went back to resurrecting hate,
With clean hands and blown nose,
Dividing the elect from the damned,
Not by merit or by fee;
The former fated by God or gene
To look exactly like me
And to clip a magazine.

Love that wounds us immortally
With a life that bends then breaks,
Leaves the earth as dreadful
As an ascetic in his cell;
Yet the martyr's wrath is just:
We earn a chronic hell
By hating gifts of dust.

ANOREXIA

Desire for God is the angels' food,
Saint Catherine said to the good;
when younger I felt the deep hunger
of such a holy pain monger.

My soul's fresh face smiled to embrace
the singular source of all grace:
God's largess drawing my goodness
as the North Sea lifts up Loch Ness.

As I grew older I turned colder
to slave than to slaveholder;
my soul would pray never to fall prey
to injustice either way.

I wanted to wait without any weight
for the end of both love and hate;
I'm no longer serene finding my queen
but losing this same fair I---.

She is what she ever was,
my head's and my heart's first cause;
pride's misdirection cost her affection,
now I am eating my own midsection.

REASONS TO BURN

Salem burned witches to purge in fire
repressed pride in Puritan desire,
righteous self-hatred in frozen souls
stoking within other-searing coals.

Berlin torched temples on Crystal Night
carrying on the contrary fight
to cauterize the new gaping wound
left by excising the ancient Good.

My flame is for an unknown goddess
that taught so careless a heart to bless
too late for my capital city
be spared the ash that knows no pity.

PASCHAL HEARTS

I touched a woman's paschal heart,
Not as healers lay on hands
Or male sea otters cuff their mates
Or idle children feel themselves
Just to pass the time,
But deadset to see her living part
Said to favor me
Quiver in its profane groove
Offending every love.

"The aorta's soft as butter,"
A surgeon once said to me,
And I saw the science in his eyes
And knew that it was so.

Our better angels we can't preserve
With chemistry or close reserve;
What is spirit decays when cooled
And, not receiving from the world,
Sends missionary pain.

And yet a light beyond the self
May thaw its clotted pulse,
Open constellated time—
Ursa Major's cup, and mine—
To catch the falling rain.

The tenderness that from afar
Descends to leave the grave ajar
Does not promise consolation,
Just itself as revelation
Of endless life in a dying pair . . .

So we love and disappear.

BUSTER IN THE BIG CITY

Young Buster Yancy bisects York Street
Daring his spirits to rise,
When tangible airs conspire with heat
To lift dust into his eyes.

Rubbing an already bloodshot ball,
He sees his salt and water;
Though vision clears to prevent a fall,
It's standing that's the matter.

Buster can perform with great finesse
Each ambulent maneuver,
And like two-wheeled bikes gone riderless,
While moving won't tip over.

He knows to keep the compass secrets:
Not to double-cross himself;
He stays within the city limits
But wanders everywhere else.

Streetsigns, yellow and black, mark deadends,
Though nothing marks the dying;
So Buster's able to round all bends
And does this without trying.

He strolls around municipal woods
And sits beneath pale birches;

In the shade of climax neighborhoods,
He sits in empty churches.

One by one the defections have come,
Leaving stone saints derelicts;
In uniform housing, no one's home:
Subdivided innocence.

No more will the thin-hipped high school girls
Go giggling across these greens,
To witness to the wide-eyed squirrels,
Feeding chestnuts, eating dreams.

ADAM'S ELATION OR THE GYNECOLOGICAL ARGUMENT FOR THE EXISTENCE OF GOD

Though I profess the old Socratic way
And look over the horizon for hope,
I admit the guilty secret today
By which I occasionally cope:
When doubt destroys calm and dread foretells storm,
I praise not Platonic but female form.

Thomas listed five ways to prove God is,
Convincing wise, consoling delicate,
Until Hume gave cosmology the biz,
And Kant showed existence no predicate.
But a sixth argument still stands time's test:
A woman's face and hip and leg and breast.

For feminine beauty to come to be,
Helping Adam love the unlovable world,
A wildly compassionate Deity
Had first to eff the ineffable Girl.
Incarnate Good, they say, once died for us,
Yet all mortals live through the uterus.

Had not Eve unique heart, mind, and voice,
Things not deducible from Adam's rib?
Are these not also reasons to rejoice
And to liberate woman from the crib?
Yes, *mens sana in corpore sano*;
But on cross and in phallus, blood must flow.

EROTIC VOICES

Hearing a silence to hang on
The self settles down in its soul:
The quiet of a carillon
After it's taken its toll.

Where breathing is text enough
And talking is uncouth;
Where tasting is a foodstuff
And eating part of youth.

Where passion is an act of grace,
Touching with both hands
The furrows on another's face,
Asking for amends.

Where seeing is a dark regret
For eyes I've brought to tears,
And consciousness an oubliette
Enlightened after years.

Then in piquant smells of summer
When a rain has turned to mist,
To the night's erotic voices
Life echoes back her gist.

FALLEN

Fallen, like the tribal hunter
Who misses a sure kill,
I trail the west wind
Back to a woman's hut
To find her still kind.

She too wears inner ashes,
Remnants of a lush green
Now graying in low fires
That burn away the roots
Of once keen desires.

Barren ages ache for children
Like phantom limbs they've lost
In some ancient holy war.
And here we know a peace
That could not cost more.

Mars lays Venus over Earth,
Turning lips then loins bloodred;
Yet across love's Hellespont
No germinal Leanders swim
Into the sacred font.

Can we keep time's secret still
Alive across the years:
Flames kindled in dry wood

Rising as censer's smoke
To make our tears good?

JEFFREY DAHMER, RIP

Sacred corpses stay incorrupt
by faith's desiccating grace;
the art of poetry does the same
for the beloved's absent face.

Hungry as a Cathar cannibal
for her blue eyes under black hair,
memories of her taste and smell
linger on the coldly vacant air.

Hate flows to meet itself
as water seeks its level;
desire without sympathy
is the torrent of the devil.

But love lifts death's veil
to kiss her drooling mouth,
emancipating us from time
like slaves in Lincoln's South.

IFS

If dawn could last all day
youth be reborn each year
love never slip away
eye never cloud with tear

If gravity could just let go
time stop taking up space
ignorance be in the know
nowhere finally get someplace

If heart could beat head's game
stomach stomach itself
ego forget its name
id stay put on a shelf

If God could become a man
the circle would be square
I might even be a fan
and learn at last to care.

FLESH IN THE THORN

Choirs' earlobes are paved with a lie
as Yeti quiet the doting and devoted
traced by cops to laws lazing on futons
as an airy riot nags us for high signs:
testing the entire bee, ox, rose, and ka.

Telic zoos lard our works with God
agley omens for a paternity ward
where dusters and lunks gibe and snap
at the life that fled docs and raxed
awakening to pine in a puce oda.

Id altars deaden the neon volts
that once animated capering frogs
to evolve past amphibian woe
and nix the single yin or yang
in one green communal leap.

Amen my cloyed unread lieges
the larvae in our wigs are rooted
in the froth of fenced pews aft of
opal gardens where thorns buttle
the dreadful auxin of the flesh.

WORD AND FLESH

What if Jesus taught also *eros*,
what he said remembered
not altered or repressed,
feeling up the cosmos,
raising embers and members,
blessing the undressed?

The Word made up with flesh,
man's to woman's primal yes,
neither immodest nor lewd
but something forever fresh
to save the horny terrorist
from murdering the nude.

Then would we have eternal life,
the heavenly kingdom come
to this very time and space?
No, there will always be mortal strife,
romantic love feel abused at home
while celibate *agape* tries to keep the peace.

BROKEN HAIKU

in climax forests
the plumed prima donnas sing
no more ecstatic

rogues dive to a lake
mating with wooden decoys
the last rite of spring

others ungravid
defy gravity alone
missing unknown nests

four wings are clipped clean
trailing pair of scattered flocks
out of formation

they drop like lead fruit
plumline to rotating crops
on rotating earth

happy, technical
hunters have let reports ring
in avian ears

behind a thatch blind
no vulnerable feathers
touch our misfired hearts

TOO DEEP FOR WORDS

Does light cast a shadow
when struck by brighter beams?
Would sleep be deeper
if untroubled by our dreams?

Are facts any truer
when known with certainty?
Should a hope be surer
when held in company?

Is the heart any keener
when we are loved in kind?
Will life be more precious
if death is not the end?

DOES DEATH?

Does death level and invalidate
Ineffectual actor with the great,
Unpublished poet with laureate,
Inconstant lover with celibate?

Do all deeds, words, and wills
Vanish forever under rank hills
Of decayed Jacks, deceived Jills,
Unsaved by prayer, politics, pills?

Entropy was not authored by you or me,
Nor Daedalus craft the wine-dark sea;
Icarus piloted his tragedy,
But you cannot blame the rat for the flea.

MULTIVERSES

is or is not, Parmenides' question,
who or what, no need to mention,
this could only be
product of fantasy

discovery or invention, nature or nurture,
sweet reason cannot name the suture
binding body and soul
part and whole

once verses affirmed the singularity
spirits enacted as human history
now parallel lines meet
as quantum dicers cheat

ancient poetry dims and ends
in eleven endless dimensions
where everything is nothing
and mind offends being

in spite of strings strumming true
eros will find another you
modern science faux artistic
our faith again polytheistic

THE TRUTH CULT

The truth cult squints
at the sick and unfit
to build with brio
a wild lie *en ami*
and weep at the union
of a dom and his wife
as the seer is soon
the dozer and a map
is ale's aide to the ear.

INDEFINITE ARTICLE

That God is not good
just for you is the shadow.
It falls in unprotesting wood,
where hawk feeds on sparrow.

Time is mind and innocent
for you in eternity's eyes.
Life is not a flawed descent,
but a failure to rise.

Crime is penance never done,
giving nothing to forgive.
Gift and giver must be one,
if the Good is to live.

These words were not written
so worlds might come to be.
Being was Love self-smitten
ere there was her and me.

A martyr is but a satyr
graced with empathy.
A pater without a mater,
she's what became of me.

How much harder is suffering,
knowing oneself to blame.

Her faith was heaven's kindling,
my pride a hellish flame.

All are had by the maelstrom,
orphaned Aiken said sighing.
But she was an angel come
to ease my way to dying.

MEMORIAL DAY: IN HONOR OF GEORGE FLOYD

All suicide is love
unrequited by the world;
if we saw it from above,
our hearts would be unfurled
to guide lost and lonely home.

All murder is hate
of our own mortality;
cruelty's knee early and late
rides the necks of you and me
but others more than some.

Let us remember on this day
those we might have blessed,
but whose lives were stripped away
while we bathed and dressed
for the burning of Rome.

SHORT STUFF: A TALE OF REDEMPTION

There was once one who knew the future course of his life, and this was the source of the greatest melancholy. So great was his melancholy that those who knew him, did not know him, and knew it, while those who did not love him, loved him, and did not like it. Or so he liked to think.

Buster always felt that the finer points of his personality were wasted on people, and this made his atheism doubly difficult. There was no all-wise Being to appreciate, but, more importantly, there was none who could truly appreciate him. Lately he had even ceased to believe in the Eternal Feminine. In matters sexual, the women he met were like French possessive pronouns: willing to take the gender and number of the objects at hand. One even spoke of her envy of a man's wet dreams. But now, with Maggie, all of this was changing.

Maggie Borah had the unconscious ability the gods once gave their favorites of communicating physically what no words could express. Just now her lambent breasts, politely supported but half-exposed by an obliging evening gown, were two bright flowers she had grown for him with their roots running clean to her heart. To want them was to want her love. Buster thought this most remarkable, the true marriage of body and soul. As for the marriage of his own mind, however, he had to admit impediments.

Impediments... apparently legion... yet actually only one: that low, dull ache that he sometimes called his "daimon" but which he suspected was really his cupidinous ego. He wanted to rule the world, or at least to finish his medical residency and then raise the dead. Until then, he walked among most people the way the risen Christ passed through walls. Maggie's great gift was momentary release from this heady existence. Buster enjoyed being with her; he wanted to thank somebody for the fact of her. But who to thank?

This was their third party together in as many nights. They had met only four days earlier at the opening of their sixth college reunion. Though classmates at Princeton, they had never crossed paths before. The cool June evening was starting to speak its romantic mind and to invite the world to love, but Buster felt the need to stall eternity for a while. "Can I get you a drink?," he asked, wanting to slip away to gather himself.

"Sure," said Maggie, in that way he already loved, "a beer... with a head on it."

Strolling to the bar, Buster wondered where his own head was. He had yet to mention he was dating someone else. A simple woman with blonde hair, one wall-eye, and deep vulnerabilities, Jane had borne his narcissism with charity for two years. Buster himself had little charity but considerable charm, and one big worry. He wanted children eventually but not necessarily a wife. Despite the best of sociobiological intentions, however, he feared that in union with Jane or anyone else he would be able to pass on neither his mind nor what was left of his heart but only his appetites, which were considerable. And then where would he be? "Two drafts please, and make 'em foamy."

Just a little beer made Buster hopelessly wistful, and he was well on his way to getting drunk. Even without drinking, he had managed to get rather maudlin over the painful death of Audrey

Hepburn, from colon cancer. He thought of the scar on Jane's stomach, from surgery for sclerosing cholangitis. He was stunned that such a thing could happen to a woman; to this day, it seemed sad and somehow indicting that women have to suffer and die like everybody else—that the shadow of death should fall even on Audrey Hepburn.

Too much Scott Fitzgerald too early? Well, there was also Rilke:

Ah, Women, that you should be moving
here, among us, grief-filled,
no more protected than we, and nevertheless
able to bless like the blessed.

Such feelings could be a school for virtue, he told himself, a Rilkean "temptation to be kind." Everyone had analogous moments of tenderness for the flesh, but what to do with them? Too much pity might cause you to "crack," like Fitzgerald, but now there was the endless freshness of Maggie's smile.

Maggie's face seemed to hover constantly before him with the supreme confidence of goodness, the complex power of feminine beauty in contrast to Jane's simple female vulnerability. Jane had suffered so severely in her life (the colongitis leading to a colostomy, a positively demonic mother) that she did not ever want to get pregnant. She doubted her own capacity for loving motherhood, and sex itself was a fearful thing. Because of so much surgery in her youth, intercourse was associated with one more threatening medical penetration. To love her was to wound her; her whole body would shake . . . Jesus, it was a shame. They had struggled so to heal this, together with more run of the mill egotisms, only to discover that she could not have children because of scarring of the fallopian tubes. The realization had broken them both in two emotionally, finally sending her to a psychiatric ward and him to the confessional of his own curtained mind.

Returning to the present, he found Maggie where he had left her—at the center of the universe—but talking to a lean, birdlike man he didn't know. Buster decided to stake a definitive claim. Handing the beers without comment to the stranger, he took Maggie's hands in his, spread her arms open cruciform, pondered, and said, "I could kill for you when you look like this." He instantly regretted the qualification, but he suspected it was true. "Who is your two-fisted drinking buddy?"

"Very funny," Maggie replied with that smile. "The man you have just insulted is my father. Meet Pershing Borah, Princeton class of '84." Buster laughed but felt the night close its mouth to him, so he pretended to be even more drunk than he was. He chugged his beer and staggered back to Jolene Hall where he had contracted for a dorm room. He fell asleep to the smell of rancid beer and alumni vomit. When Maggie called him the next day, he knew he would spill his own blood for her. This was a something new, the beginning of the beginning.

SECOND TIMOTHY

My eyes reflect a foreign light
Though they do not see the sun—
Not a torch or harvest moon,
Just a lover none too soon
Come of age and innocence,
Come to plead for tolerance
In my own behalf.

My feet are bound by memory
Of wrong before and after,
But as it made another smile
To wash him with expensive oil,
So she lessens now and then
The judgment upon older men
With her sweet appeal.

My hands at no communion hold
A finer vessel than she is;
They give far less than they get
Deep within this oubliette
Where sobriety's the wine of grace
But passion's for this human face
As I drink to her.

Two hearts together surely know
Formality's a proof of love;
If two minds apart can just hope

For present faith's eternal scope,
A child will spring from her and me
Who sets his future parents free
To bring about the past.

For we are panders passing time
Who cannot bear ourselves,
Until a virgin bears our son
And we conceive his will.

II

Philia and Humor

HAIKU FOR WENDELL BERRY

in over-cut woods
the red-faced warblers sing to
Standing Room Only

king eiders descend
mating with wooden decoys
as the down flies up

one dove ungravid
defies gravity alone
nests but in my eye

would-be butterfly
kamikaze without nerve
is uprooted man

your planting at home
Henry County, Kentucky
cultivates the world

love a burnt oak leaf
imperfect as a person
and you shed yourself

AN ERA'S WARMEST EYE

Poems felt between the legs
Not etched before the eyes
Possess an intensity
Not to be despised.

Sublimer still of course:
Mens sana in corpore sano;
But who has so composed himself
In this *Domini anno*?

I could say I cannot say
Who wrote such poems yesterday
That neither time nor space abates;
But it was William Butler Yeats.

The influence of his anxiety
Was Maud Gonne's lasting legacy;
Our poems to his still refer:
Echoes in the deep heart's core.

Would we see his like again,
Could we stay our horsemen,
If we knew the sufferings
That warmth of vision brings?

ORLANDO FURIOSO 2

Twenty-five score years ago
Christian chivalry rhymed its fears.
The epic *Orlando Furioso*
wrung out Europe's tears,
leaving Ludovico Ariosto
a model for his peers:
How to make the Saracen
take it always on the chin.

Charlemagne sent each paladin
to scour for Christ the East,
douse the lamp of Aladdin,
slaughter the Arab beast,
let alien blood gladden
the holy ones at feast.
Thus did they repeal
the agape meal.

Now the gaze that can only kill
and the soul unable to die
turn on a different infidel
whose name is "you" and "I."
Only true lovers are mortal,
compassionate their eye.
Whether gay or straight
fury's twin is hate.

Florida, America, we rightly mourn,
and the murderer was ever dead.
But let a new peace be born
as the innocents' names are read
into our opened heart, a horn-
book dear as wine and bread.
The world knows us better
when Spirit rules letter.

BLOOMSDAY

When John Milton died of gout
the lamp of English lit went out.
John Dryden was very clever,
but he held a grudge forever;
he could not bring in the sheaves
while reaping mistress Anne Reeves.

So our evolving human nature,
invented as Hamlet by Shakespeare,
had only steadily gotten worse
since losing Eden in blank verse,
until Walt Whitman began to yearn
and America had money to burn.

Human poets father anxiety
in any children who would be
held in more timeless acclaim,
like King Herod vowing slaughter
of every son of every daughter
who might be graced by flame.

Only God can be so kenotic
to coin a Word unerotic
inscribed in a book of dust;
the holy gift is complete,
a writer need not compete,
for in His mettle we trust.

THE GENIUS OF KEY WEST

"The mind is the end and must be satisfied,"
Said the genius of Key West,
Not Hemingway, but the other one,
The meteorologist of the imagination,
Wallace Stevens, unsurpassed in facility
With words, words insuring other words,
The hyper-romantic terminus
Of our literature from Emerson on,
Edwards notwithstanding,
The eclipse of the divine even at Yale.

Why then do I pine for the Word,
Not happiness but holiness?

"The world is myself. Life is myself."
Not even Whitman could have said it better,
Or worse, prouder, louder, the lauder of pride
As secular saint, happy as a clam
Seasoning himself as chowder, powder
Magazine of the mental fort
Rifled canons reduce and may set ablaze,
Like Pulaski in Savannah Harbor,
Dying for the noble revolution
Of our post-colonial consciousness.

Why then do I fear despair,
Not anxiety but sin?

Not even in southernmost Florida is the receiver
The reception, a tan the light. Currents and corneas
Refract, but they make deities out of sun worshippers
Only in the eyes of airbrushed magazine editors
Selling the imago femina to Connecticut Yankees
On business vacations from snow and sobriety,
While wives back home in too-real Hartford
Put the children to bed to dream of dromedaries,
Dads, guppies, and God,
Not of their own making.

Stevens' poems are a fireworks display,
Sonorous and combusting, celebrating survival,
Yet all but invisible, ignited at midday,
Lost in the sunlight they mimic and rival.

I will go fishing off the coastal lee,
And I shall hope soon to be hooked,
Not in Mexico's Gulf but Galilee's Sea;
The former has been over-booked.

FOR JOHN KEATS

Cedar waxwings do not sing,
Telling no territorial tale
Yet pitying Keats for the sting
Of his silenced nightingale.
Where is more beautiful truth . . .
The linnet in bright plumage,
Caged for its romantic voice
And dying in its youth,
Or the albatross of vetust age
That does not lament or rejoice?

Death descends posthumously for aesthetes;
Life climbs prenatally the Spanish Steps;
Outside the poet's Roman window a heart beats
That hails existence from unknowing depths.
A phobic crown burned the phthisic boat-bed
To consume consumption in public flames;
Today's tourists take their sunny selfies,
Oblivious to the suffering once overhead
Of a private soul obsessed with proper names,
Like queen-less, contented honey bees.

Which is the greater moral share,
Biblical *agape* or Greek eudaimony?
Both are virtuous and self-aware,
Beyond the crowd's dull harmony.
But the dialectic of chance and fate

Asks of Keats' and our free choices:
Whose the good, whose the purpose?,
As finite and fallibly we wait
For other poets with stronger voices,
Only to find they won't speak to us.

The fiery particle passed with *le petit caporal*
Undone by the Russian winter;
He knew a quarter century to be his all
Without an Italian summer.
Some names are written in blood,
Leviathans of force and nullity,
Deathless devils to the race,
Embodying dread of the good,
Too weak for humility,
Too shameless for grace.

Every chilled or fevered cell a portal
Loving beauty into his lost time,
Keats for mortality became immortal
Teaching a bird, a pot, and us to rhyme.
Do not mourn the name writ in water:
The bride-less sire had his offspring,
And the fiancée married another man.
Neither fame nor happiness was the matter,
But saved from nothingness by Being
To uphold the other's trembling hand.

JUST A SMILE AT AUDEN

Too well-bred to be sad or ill,
Too word-drunk to be sane,
Wystan Hugh ascends your will
To the apex of your pain.

He startles you and steals your pearl,
Though this is not his mission;
He is good's portal to your world;
You can only thank the physician.

He cures a sickness you do not have
And worsens one you do;
He shakes the stillness of the grave
And opens the tomb in you.

You want the corpse at once withdrawn,
Not fathomed deeper and deeper;
You are midnight impatient for dawn;
He is your brother's keeper.

A prophet channels evanescent grace,
Not knowing who or how or whether,
Awakens screaming like the fevered Keats
Still alive yet written in water.

But when you die and die again
To happiness and hope,

He will by your bier remain
And bless you like a pope.

WITHOUT ENEMY OR IMMORTALITY?

(In honor of Richard Rorty)

Ancient heroes taught us to cope,
Living on what we hate or hope:
For now, the enemy;
Later, immortality.
But these two have started to fray;
I, for one, can keep neither at bay.

Jesus aimed to exorcise ill-will,
Showing us how the soul can still;
But the sheathing of Peter's sword
Was tied to heavenly reward.
As pagan Nietzsche so rudely brayed,
Christians insist on being well-paid.

Can we forego each classic crutch,
Not hating or hoping much,
Leavening time with liberal irony,
Finding refuge from melancholy
In family, friends, and literature?
To tell the truth, I am not sure.

THE ART OF POETRY

The art of poetry is darkness
made light by invented accident:
joy under juniper trees
after rain has seasoned the leaves
into libidinous perfume
hiding us from ourselves,
gravity of an October moon
growing surfers' white tides
like a chubby old man
forgetting to trim his beard
taken by children for Santa Claus.

Ready, aim, fire . . .grazed by grace
in ancient cooking and killing;
atlatl or ax, muzzleloader or breech
will fill a pot or plot with meat,
the beginning and end
of axolotls, apes, and us.
Who provides the beans and bullets
for our stomachs and our Sten guns?
Our societies and our sonnets
are Downs babies raised up
by an action, not an event.

THE FOUND POET: JAMES TATE, RIP

I read you today for three and a half hours,
but it seemed like three hours
and thirty minutes

yesterday.
Like *Finnegans Wake*,
only less intelligible,

your verses moved,
Bolshoi impala,
hares in heat,

leaping down my throat
before I could gag
on blood-rare absurdity

and spit out the truth
with fur on it:
what our species lived on

before we got reason
and forgot poetry.

SONG FOR GAIL

She changes the linen on hotel beds,
A job she got when twenty-five,
And though I've met some quicker heads
I've never seen any finer eyes.

It is unmeasured downcast looks,
Broken in two by a toothy smile,
That moves the author of these books
And gives him poetry awhile.

She stands so still, alive to the touch
Of another's spirit upon her own;
Yet her silence is singing far too much
For his ears of flesh and bone.

So should I smile and condescend
To explore the vices in a wink,
Exchanged between myself and friends
Who neither feel nor think?

No, for the very flowers would not endure it.

And now she asks me if I like to swim . . .

WHO WILL WAIT WITH POETRY?

I found an old book of poetry,
My mother's at twenty-two,
Finishing college in '45,
As the subsiding Second War divided
Red East and bluesy West, but reunited
Combatant men and civilian women.

She had marked to "memorize"
Two lines from Frost's "Birches":
"I'd like to get away from earth awhile
And then come back to it and begin over."

If a son thinks of his mother,
It is as the singular earth itself,
Nourishing and ever-present,
At times too damned ubiquitous,
Like gravity or dark matter,
So this posed a strange maternal metaphysic.

Had she gotten away? If so,
How had the earth fared without her?
She married my father in '48,
Was that her beginning over
Or just the opposite:
A lost opportunity, resulting in me?

Fast forward a lifetime to 2015,
And women are to be sent into combat
In all branches of the American military.
When they return in body bags,
Earth to earth, no male duty to protect,
Who will wait with poetry?

Who will return to the earth without a sword?

COUNTING

A girl of two runs wild at mass,
ancient priestess full of joy;
her father wisely lets her pass,
himself once more a boy.

She scales the altar of my soul
with steps five inches long,
redeeming my archaic dole
with a vision of nothing wrong.

An Asian woman young and blind
leaves a lecture on Plato's king;
I open the door to be kind,
but she does not ask a thing.

She smiles at her dog and my voice,
but I am the one with a guide,
leading to where our hearts rejoice
at courage and innocent pride.

CYRUS'S CHILDREN

Palmyra is erect no more,
Ancient columns of the god of war,
Blasted long before they fell
By frightened sons Oedipal.

Jews and Christians too recall
Wrestling with the ghost of Baal,
Yet there is no victory in
Cyrus slain by his children.

The Lion of Al-lāt would eat
Straw instead of gazelle meat,
If the hearts of Wahhabi Sunni
Heed the words of Mawlānā Rumi.

WHITTAKER CHAMBERS, RIP

Derving bells of Notre Dame
Chime still the sad alarm
That cost a hunchback
His sense of hearing.
Once tyranny was nearing.

We watched a private little man
Flayed upon a witness stand
And testified to his flesh
Secret lesions in our own.
Beneath our backs he was the bone.

Gone is he, almost forgotten,
Who played for us the part of Laughton
Shouting from the cracked facade
Of the modern West:
"Sanctuary to the last!"

If on this world that never ends
A Cold Friday again descends,
Will no prepossessing sanctus
Call the dispossessed by name?
This to us is all the same.

KENTUCKY PARADOXES

White on brown in the Bluegrass,
Christmas snow near Bardstown
Drapes Lincoln's cabin,
Merton's coffin,
With swaddling shroud.

The ugly giant without malice
Rose from Sinking Spring
To free the slaves,
Bind the Union,
With martial beauty.

The chaste brother, already father,
Dismounted seven stories,
Vowing silence,
Writing volumes,
To teach us how to love.

Of the same commonwealth,
Jefferson Davis unmade his name:
Handsome, witty,
Yet blind to black pain,
He declared a bankrupt independence.

Another near miss to morals
Would Carry A. Nation
Up to temperance

With hatchetations:
The divorcee as reformer.

What paradoxes of our border-state
On this December eve,
Margin of the new year,
Are slouching toward Louisville
To be born, or buried?

ICONS IN OLD LOUISVILLE

On a single block in Louisville,
adjacent to the Seelbach Hotel,
frozen icons of good and evil
in shade of Assumption Cathedral.

The Dalai Lama and Thomas Merton
smile at the oblivious pedestrians
as they shop, swear, sorrow, and shine
without eternity or time.

Across the street, Al Capone and his cronies
bet on cards and the ponies,
while Scott Fitzgerald turned Jazz Age ironies
to tragi-comic stories.

A past generation will send help
the last minute of the eleventh hour:
our postmodern yelp
for plows that will not scour.

THE PACIFIC

Former soldiers and would-be naturalists
insouciant surfers and suicidal poets
the chaste, barren, and prolific
seek a route to the Pacific.

From the Falls of the Ohio
Lewis and Clark projected Jefferson;
carried to Galapagos shores
unhieing Darwin rewrote Genesis.

Hart Crane made it to the Gulf of Mexico
where his Muse became the undertow
that shall pull down all bridges
and wash away Melville's grave.

BLOWING OUR QI

God and the devil create nuns
who warn fools with holy cooee
and veto the diet of pied bullshit
of roadies on a jag . . .
ants, boars, gnus, and me,
tare of the zoa,
as we trip along the dale
blowing our qi for xu.

SENDING REGRETS

Greet regret with a grin
over and over again,
or you will find contrition
a terminal condition:
death's first act.

The end of all beginnings,
the loss of any winnings,
the face of life once fair
scowling scarred by despair:
fiction now fact.

LOVING ANNE SEXTON

She tried to commit,
was committed,
recommitted,
wrote herself into a corner,
ink fumes heady as Delphi,
telic yet toxic,
an asp drawing out its own venom.

She saw too much life,
lived too much vision,
until she had to die,
but she waited,
holding her breath,
the opposite of hibernation,
sweating whenever the cat moved.

Insanity, handsome and cruel,
raped her like a prinking Nazi officer
quoting Friedrich Nietzsche,
leaving her a dog eating feces,
still she dropped postcards
from the train to Auschwitz
until work set her free.

Showers were a Shoah sham,
yet she deloused herself and I AM
before asphyxiating,

her sleep and our waking,
in a garage massed with myriad.

Anne Sexton had to die;
so do you and I.
May we take the time
to make our suffering rhyme,
though the grave be a period.

That is how she loved us,
in spite of her abuse,
in spite of her abuse . . .
Futility that found a use,
Kierkegaard without God's muse.

WAS HEIST MARTIN HEIDEGGER

Imagine Socrates cared about his public reputation,
Feared death, and threw in with the Thirty Tyrants,
His dialectical skills beyond all but imitation
Yet often confusing obscurantism for science,
Greek language and Athenian soil for gods.

Even those who talk of Plato
May stand you in the sun
And let the heat undo you
Until you are undone.

SOME ENGLISH LANGUAGE WRITERS

Some English language writers
Make you proud to use the tongue;
They silence crowns and miters:
Locke, Paine, Jefferson.

Others set erotic fire
To the body and the voice,
Burning shame upon a pyre:
Byron, Lawrence, Joyce.

Still others touch the soul
In its eternal isolation,
Freeing from time's gaol:
Wordsworth, Keats, Dickenson.

Yet highest is the mansion
That translates human hates
Into divine compassion:
Shakespeare, Lincoln, Yeats.

HAIKU FOR AUTUMNAL YALE

Jonathan Edwards
despised humanity's fall
I love New England's

When at Halloween
Eli elms don Princeton orange
New Haven Green isn't

Autumnal Yale served
the last feasting of my soul
I now fast on poems

A TOURIST PETS THE SPHINX

I saw a cat from the deck of Sun Boat III,
The way God might look down at me:
A creature once venerated by Queen Nefertari
Now scrounges for scraps of cheese or calamari,
And no one cares to mummify her.

Humanity too peaks and declines
As poignantly as Egyptian felines:
We once aspired to be regal and holy,
To stalk eternity like the Sphinx, slowly.
But now time is a nullifier.

Contempt and despair are not the answers,
Rather leap and laugh like Nubian dancers,
Know Seth the Hippo yet will be chained,
The Nile flooded, Washington drained,
Isis the Great Mother no more forlorn crier.

With gravity every material thing falls,
Yet the voice of the Good still soothes and calls,
Sustaining us like tourists led by Fetiche,
Who keeps bodies and souls on her loving leash
Until grace teaches us to fall higher.

CATECHISM

Protestantism is the beach hotel
you visit on spring break
that doesn't take kids or dogs;
Catholicism the snow-covered cottage
where you were born
and want to die.

The roof is sagging
and the plumbing leaks,
but memories haunt the place,
and the fireplace warms
body and soul
with charms unchosen.

ANTI-HEROES

What if Hemingway were assassinated
And Lincoln a suicide,
Gandhi always ate 'til sated
And Elvis self-denied?

What if Zelda were not insane
And Jeanne d'Arc certifiable,
Franco lost the war in Spain
And Hitler loved the Bible?

What if Moses made the promised land
And Lindy crashed at sea,
Lennon never formed a band
And Kierkegaard liked company?

What if Washington were a liar
And Clinton told the truth,
Isaac died on the pyre
And Keats survived his youth?

What if King were violent
And Ali did not box,
Eve rebuffed the serpent
And Helen weren't a fox?

What if Malcolm made no Hajj
And Oswald moved to Cuba,

Henry Ford drove a Dodge
And Heifetz played the tuba?

What if Einstein did not see the light
And Oedipus were not blind,
Jesus were not on God's right
And I were brave and kind?

ANCIENT GRAFFITI

There would have been no Trojan War
Had Priam a Trojan wore;
Then Hecuba does not Paris bear,
Nor Helen her *parus* bare;
But Achilles is still a heel.

THE END OF THE ORAL TRADITION

How often did I kiss you,
a part of the loving face,
and smile with you at life,
brilliant and white!

Admittedly, you were wayward –
it took years to straighten you out –
and you cut others uncaring
what became of the corpse.

But I could count on you,
and you never left me,
until that night at the Trondheim café
when you departed over a crust of pizza.

Now you are an object to me,
dead and detached, a curiosity;
I don't know where you are;
you are no longer personal.

I will never again grin at a girl,
flashing you like a great price pearl;
I am old, you are yellow,
I can't even place you under my pillow.

A BRIEF HISTORY OF SCIENCE

Numerology counted as math
When it added a zero;
Mythology made history
When it subtracted the hero.

Astrology foretold astronomy
When stars debunked the fable;
Alchemy served up chemistry
When the elements sat at table.

Yet physics can't conceive biology,
And the soul still takes the veil;
Life is more than matter in motion,
And love weighs less on a scale.

A LIBERAL HISTORY OF WESTERN THOUGHT

I. Rahner as a Christianized Heidegger

II. Heidegger as a Secularized Kierkegaard

III. Kierkegaard as a Christianized Kant

IV. Kant as a Secularized Luther

V. Luther as a Christianized Aquinas (sic)

VI. Aquinas as a Secularized Augustine

VII. Augustine as a Christianized Plato

VIII. Plato as Anticipating Jesus

IX. Conclusion: The European Philosophical Tradition Is God's Footnote to Plato (cf. Whitehead)

RULES FOR SAINT GEORGE RENTERS

Don't swerve to miss the black bears
Bounding across a dark road;
They will only smile at your fears
And scoff at your moral code.

Turn out the lights for the turtles,
Hatchlings on their way to the sea;
Human inventions are hurdles
For pilgrims like them and like me.

Put no key under the mat for the crab,
He has one of his own 'neath the sand;
Like a religiously insulted Arab,
His claw will shake its fist at your hand.

Leave the sky ajar for the heron,
Great, blue, without suffering;
Human limbs fertile or barren
Evolved from her ancient wing.

Rise early to fish in the cold rain;
It will be the peak of a splendid stay.
Even if you wake with an old brain,
Your youth will be caught like a ray.

Bow down at last to the bald eagles,
Wilder than any seal or state;

American citizens and illegals,
We share *their* real estate.

A JEWISH JOYCE KILMER

An ancient tree need not see
very much geography,
for it touches sky and earth
in the homeland of its birth.

It sends roots deep into soil,
shedding leaves with autumn mohel;
sun and rain are all it needs,
breeze the rabbi of its seeds.

The tree brightens every place
with its multi-colored face,
making axmen in each state
green with envy, red with hate.

Jews were never meant to be
sedentary as a tree,
still give thanks on Arbor Day
for the planting of Yahweh.

TO FLORENCE TO SEE THE MOON

To Florence to see the moon,
the Renaissance comes too soon
for a post-modern in synch
with red nature and instinct.

I don't count on Beatrice
to raise me from caprice
as bubbles in prosecco
lift the pragmatic ego.

I live as pure gravity;
matter knows no depravity;
and I am forever one
with the multiverse pagan.

Christ walked the Galilean Sea,
but he is still Jesus to me.
As he asked, I don't weep for him:
all regret is just a whim.

THE AVUNCULAR VISITOR

It comes upon you like a distant uncle
who has promised—threatened really –
to visit you for years now
but you don't believe him
until one evening he appears at your door
with an embarrassed smile and two bags.

You can't not let him in
he is one of the family after all
part of you and yours
but you don't like him much
hardly recognize him in fact
though he looks vaguely like your father.

You show him to the guest bedroom
with a private bath on the basement level
but he prefers to sleep on the sofa
in the upstairs den to be near the television
and cd player and to be able to raid the fridge
without climbing stairs.

You try to explain your routine to him
and assure him he is welcome but needs
to keep to the living space you assign him
yet he does not seem to hear you and wanders
the house late at night leaving dirty dishes all over
and upsetting your wife with his thoughtlessness.

When he says he will help with the housework
you know he is lying and couldn't lift a broom
even if he tried cause of his bad back
so you cancel your regular racquetball game
to keep him company and accept life has changed
but, as they say, it beats dying.

ETERNAL LIFE

move the oceans to be wet
ask the Jews not to forget
command a lilac to bloom
confine a hermit to his room.

press a diamond to be hard
cast Shakespeare as the Bard
kindle the sun to be hot
count on zero to be naught.

prod thoroughbreds to run
hope Gen Xers have fun
help hummingbirds beat the air
urge angels not to despair.

force the universe to expand
pile the deserts full of sand
invite darkness to spend the night
do not exceed the speed of light.

teach a Stoic not to mind
inspire a saint to be kind
conjecture life is a guess
you will never know death.

IN SICKNESS AND IN HEALTH

Cancer is the body's way of divorcing the soul,
claiming irreconcilable differences;
conscience is the soul's way of wedding the body,
taking responsibility for its weaknesses.

We need a pandemic of patience,
a counter-COVID of charity,
in which a contagious goodness
reconciles the flesh and the spirit.

Personal virtue depends on this,
the American experiment in democracy,
the Olympic ethos of irenic competition too:
a new catholic saintliness,
just like the old one.

But I am an uranophobe
not up to the eternal task;
my inner cleric exchanged his robe
for an Autenrieth mask.

DESPAIR

He unwas the moment he lost her is
though he lived on might for years
trying to strike a compromise
between suicide and tears.
Love gone or come too late
an amputee's haunting pain
abused affection turned to hate
a bullet to the brain.
Himself victim and executioner
despite caveats from Camus
he gnawed being and time from her
a venomous male shrew.
    Thank you, Lord, for the crucifix,
    but some hearts even God can't fix.

THE BIRTH OF THE LAMB

I wear a watch that has stopped
a yearning that yeans eternity.
Ardent aliens joust at our border
beneath a crimpy American flag
while overt piracy strips the leys
where the sacred cow would graze
and reens rush to glut the seas
with tides of torts and retorts.

"I'm just kidding,"
said the right-eyed wink of God
when he created mortality,
but left-eye-winking man
took him seriously
and invented evil to compensate.

I flane into the flames of self . . .
I must go mad or know God . . .

III

Agape and Forgiveness

ONE SURPASSING POEM

Mundane halls reek with infinities
Yule logs like guard rails convene debs
goons on pogos roost on the fen
shooting selfies and diving into REM
while the odor of cars breaks my jaw
and sets me lugging words to the sky
to write another ordinary day.

One surpassing poem
singular creation of a universe
worlds banging from words
in the beginning was the verb
energy condensing into nouns
like supermassive black holes
from which nothing escapes
gerunds the genes of galaxies
adjectives for our agonies.

One surpassing poem
second round with the Serpent
ego too blasé to rise and walk
squirming like a sleeper in nightmare
crossing only himself in the dark
endlessly begging a new sentence
from a jury more than just
for the line of Cain and Abel
effing the ineffable.

One surpassing poem
a covenant with Earth
requiting its archaic dust
with the evolving names
of *'hesed* and *agape*
thrice blessing the trinity of love
that enforces the duty to live
for the mortal frame of guilt
time and language have built.

Descend gift that transcends falls
and give regret no reprieve.
Let me overhear the echoing word
of silence in the deafening woods
lighted by the voice of stars.
Grace my grave with an epitaph
composed before I was born
read by children whose first breath
was their abortion and our death.

As the Nile once flooded the Sahara
with eternity's sacred blue lotus
give me preternatural powers
ordinary as the veins on a leaf
or the alluvial soil of a civilization.
Then will I rejoice like the first papyrus
receiving the first hieroglyph
and preserve in memory's myrrh
the beauty and the love of Her.

MY PRAYER OF SAINTE SIMONE

To philosophize without Wisdom
to win without Nike's joy
to attend blind, deaf, and dumb
to play when you are the toy.

To hate finding no satisfaction
to wait with no expectancy
to love losing the name of action
to be you but never me.

To hope where there is no future
to hunt when you are the prey
to operate with no suture
tonight without today.

To worship outside all pews
to report for duty unfit
to reiterate eternity's news
to refuse "*anathema sit.*"

To recall the cross on Christmas
to suffer a baby to be born
to believe in what never was
to spurn the crowd's glad scorn

To be liberated yet not free
to be healthy and diseased

to die for immortality
to live once life has ceased.

This is Good Friday's cup
when we are all named Pontius
by grace we've fallen up
and Easter become conscious.

PETITION

Speak my soul into love
that I might hear your word;
subvert my heart from above
that I might sheathe my sword.

Read my mind into prayer
that I might see new birth;
dip my tongue in your bloody fare
that I might taste its worth.

Sear my flesh in the holy flame
that anneals where self cremates;
let your Spirit lift all that's lame
and abase all that hates.

HOLINESS

Holiness is not despotic,
coercing a bended knee;
the heart of God is kenotic,
breaking for you and me.

Bookburners never suspect
words are already on fire;
we are the willing genuflect
Jewish embers should inspire.

This is the Messiah's Word,
why he suffered and died:
if you listen, you will be heard;
to be resurrected, be crucified.

Live forever every day,
grace's bottomless delf;
heaven is then serendipity,
and eternity takes care of itself.

EASTERN ORTHDOXY

The ivy-covered huts where the yogis live
Are eyed by squads of noisy eagles
For whom dew is fusel oil
And there is no flight from fire.
When the evolved opal takes the coders
Off the grid and into the lair of life,
Then the ruins of Kiev will cure the saints
Of their cloistered holiness.

TO THE ETERNAL MOTHER

Wet wind washes the moon away
from a softened slate-blue sky;
science lost its mind the first day
matter mattered more than I.

The sun sole darling of Akhenaten
and Plato's proxy for good
is now the species' prime carcinogen
and the spark of Berkeley's wood.

Pragmatists deem disenchantment crucial
for evolving Darwin's thumb;
romantics lament words inaudible
to the ever deaf and dumb.

But holiness will not forget the one
who remembers gratefully
the eternal mater who has foregone
abortion of you and me.

DIVINE FERTILITY

If God were infertile
He'd not incarnate be,
and we would call cloning
true immortality.

If the world were a copy
of a circle's boundary,
Herr Nietzsche would be faith
instead of heresy.

Omniscience alone can design
perpetual motion machines
that we forever dream about
in periodic magazines.

Inwardness in each of us
finds epiphany in pain:
I feel ergo I am
a mind before a brain.

Light makes very good time
from the sun to my face,
but truth is still delayed
by my taking up space.

Don't wink at the woman
or claim her as your girl,

it is more than enough
to know she bears a pearl.

INSUFFICIENT UNTO YESTERDAY IS THE GOOD THEREOF

The lilies are not themselves today,
working and weaving,
forced to smell us
as they decline to bloom,
sucking the oxygen from the room,
envying Solomon's
soul.

The birds go to barn dances
or starve on the wing,
driven daft by Daphne,
not Apollo's but Hitch's,
resenting sons of bitches
who don't need to fly
south.

Flora and fauna are fossils,
fetuses of the mind,
pointing back at conception
of genius in genes,
of selves in seeds,
lamenting the long night ere
nous.

Life and time are kindling
stoking Being's flame;

bookburners never suspect
silence is also on fire
awaiting words to inspire
and melt matter's mute
youth.

MATTERS OF LIFE AND DEATH

I.

Live as though you are already dead,
and you will not die prematurely.

Die as though you are living still,
and you will resuscitate another.

Mend as though you were never ill,
and you will pass away obscurely.

Smile at gray hairs on your bowed head,
and you will be your father's mother.

II.

Epicurus parsed death no parting,
an intransitive verb, nothing
to feel so nothing to fear
for the self we hold so dear.

He forgot time's deceiving
will not let us be Being,
nor give a moment's peace
to eternity's loss of innocence.

Keats consoled by Chatterton's arsenic
and inspired by his candid despair,
the name written in water is classic
but not the one written in air.

Epic feelers like Scott Fitzgerald
with nostalgic pining oddly herald
a new day for the creative word
no longer with or as God.

How many Genies have died mute,
kept like pets whose whining is cute,
assuring free speech makes us kings
all other lives may be treated as things?

I am not I from day to day,
inner child won't come out to play,
so I will dread my lost mind
and find your minding unkind.

III.

I have been in the camp for several months now, how many I'm not sure. I came, like all the others, via a dark and winding rail journey. The further we travelled, the slower the car seemed to roll and the more cramped it felt. My first weeks here, I was numb. Lately, I have begun to feel more. Last Friday, they came and took my brother away, I presume to his death. In our barracks, there is no air, and we breathe our own urine and feces. When the person beside me coughs, I wake up and kick her.

I often wonder if I will get out alive. The wider world seems to be full of stalwart friends and inscrutable enemies. Why don't the forces of good intervene to save us? We are so vulnerable and too weak to protect ourselves.

There is a stir in the camp this morning. Something momentous is happening. Are the liberators coming? No, it is the executioner! He grabs my head with his metallic hands and squeezes tight. My skull fractures.

I am being aborted . . .

THE EARWIG

An earwig crawled across my book of verse,
no larger than three letters on the page;
my first thought made my finger her hearse,
but I vaguely sensed she was a sage.

Un-self-consciously animate,
moved the graceful timeless being;
her heedless form nature's opiate
blurred and blessed my silently seeing.

She wandered as if a wayward child,
oblivious of me and Keats' "Urn";
my heart grew so still and mild,
I knew what I had to learn:

Not a thing that lives is not loved;
not a poem that is writ is unread;
our sky has another sky above;
and even death can hold up its head.

SIMPLE GIFTS

Pen me in prisons with no walls
Set me free to wander nowhere
Let me hear my own footfalls
As I stand on the empty air

Count the days in each hour
Span the space between red
Remove the tonsils of a flower
Convince a mummy he's dead

Show my blindness the full moon
Fill the emptiness of all hate
Wake me before yesterday noon
And don't make eternity wait

ALL SAINTS DAY: A GOTHIC ROMANCE

Is *agape* the Beauvais Cathedral of the virtues?
Vaulted ceiling grasping ambivalently for heaven,
praise and pride, monument and money,
without a nave where laity might live,
walls too thin to support the burden of stoning
and an apse without buttress enough for its cross.

Piety ascending from the heart
is routed by the gravity of bowels
and avails a smug comedy viler
than the cozy flab of prayerless hours
in a ghetto of Dionysian denial,
as tourists flock to see the collapse.

THE IMMACULATE CONCEPTION CONCEIVED

She carries immortality in her eye,
No man can look upon her face and die;
She reverses time's all-corrupting flow
And brings us back the eternal now
. . . giving birth, even in death.

Mother with children, may you gather
Forever before the loving Father
Our best hopes, worst fears,
All that puts soul in arrears
. . . to pride and to wealth.

And let your prayers be heard
By the Spirit and the Word,
Who know the blessing of the flesh
Only by your maternal kindness
. . . to a miscarried earth.

THE LOVE OF GOD

The love of God is tried and true;
The love of God fails me and you;
The love of God knows all that is;
The love of God forgets this.

The love of God transcends time and space;
The love of God prefers our place;
The love of God unites the world;
The love of God is a flag unfurled.

The love of God is His Son;
The love of God is barren;
The love of God invents safe sex;
The love of God is Oedipus Rex.

The love of God speaks loudest in silence;
The love of God is mute before violence;
The love of God would have us pray;
The love of God would have them prey.

The love of God forgives the whore;
The love of God is the dog of war;
The love of God fires the universe;
The love of God fills the hearse.

The love of God redeems each sin;
The love of God takes the sucker in;

The love of God gives the prophets;
The love of God takes the profits.

The love of God opens the grave;
The love of God makes others slave;
The love of God serves not mammon;
The love of God spills oil on Eden.

The love of God inspires hope;
The love of God obeys the pope;
The love of God goes to the cross;
The love of God wants to be boss.

The love of God conceives immaculate Mary;
The love of God paints the Father hairy;
The love of God gives life to us;
The love of God aborts the fetus.

The love of God binds Eve to Adam;
The love of God splits e from atom;
The love of God saves both Adam and Eve;
The love of God offers no one reprieve.

God's love for us is a freeing grace;
Our love for God is a fugitive race.

INWARD AND OUTWARD

Prim loins reap no genes
but inherit the wit that waits
on the ghost in the machine,
the unjust guillotine,
patient as a deposed queen
with real divine right.

Primal gods do not avow
anything but themselves,
toiling unrested by the years,
relishing talons and spears,
bleeding the rite that cures
no one right or wrong.

Oaring to a roofless verity
fires the new and true divine,
as sane elites wince at dry pubs
and raft home on their own spit.

Oafing through our days,
the rest of us go cold turkey
on the sacred wine of youth
and lie down in rootless dirt.

Oating the horse of the soul on
Trappist beer, bread, and breath
is now the only remedy for
an anorexic sage and age.

THE AMNIOTIC SACK

modern mind mechanistic
submerged Elysian Fields
monkish manner mystic
evermore yields

atavistic Argonauts
home from fleecing foes
awaken angels and archangels
to eternity of woes

happiness hunting humans
forget how just to live
'hesed heeding Hebrews
give and give and give

ground given grain
is placed inside a bowl
baby aborted before birth
is searching for a soul

trying to think timelessly
even while in time
Heraclitian heroes
emerge out of rhyme

. . . .

we think we know in advance
what human life is
then inquire whether a fetus
meets our dead standards

because a being does not move
is not yet breathing or aware
it is not one of us
and can (un)easily be destroyed

love, in contrast, learns
from the evolving creature
what living is, celebrating
it as a revelation

can we distinguish
a product for sale
from a good gift
to our poverty?

BERNINI'S SAINT TERESA

Teresa, ecstatic ecdysiast,
Virtuous folds of habit recast
Interior castle of body and soul
In melting wax for impish angel
Arrow raised for penetration

Divine grammar, word into flesh,
Subjects and objects enmesh
Warp and woof space and time
While artists pantomime
The transverberation

Cold feet, last to liquefy,
Walk on water in the sky
Golden grace explodes above
In God, erotic and agapic love
Are forever and ever one

Gian Lorenzo Bernini's "The Ecstasy of Saint Teresa" (1647–52), in the Cornaro Chapel of the Church of Santa Maria della Vittoria in Rome

SAINT CATHERINE'S SILK BAG

Is time the soothing saga of history
or a belch rude and inarticulate?
Is space a tapestry exquisitely woven
or a hole torn in nothingness?

Am I, a moment of matter,
a message truer than myself
or a creature of Another's faith
in fable and in fabric?

Transport my soul to Beatitude, Catherine,
as Raymond carried your severed head
to the pilgrim's Basilica of Siena,
where time and space meet to pray.

A FRIDAY DIALOGUE

Soul: Silence to silence beauty speaks,
    as this holy morning breaks;
    let me, like the good thief, hear
    Paradise whispering in my ear.

Self: Deeper than language is my heart,
    botched beyond all healing art,
    an ineffable dread despair
    no thought or feeling can repair.

Soul: All communication of the Word
    tells a story already heard,
    even as the resurrecting Good
    must pass through our guts as food.

Self: All life resolves to perpetual scream,
    like Kant's dog, less than a dream:
    "911 . . . What is your emergency?"
    Me, me, me, me, me!"

Soul: Yet could we know the foulest waste
    if earth weren't salted with the taste
    of someone or –thing from above
    suffering that we might learn to love?

Self: Left on the cross to die and decay,
    Jesus' body did not fly away;

you pasteurize it as bread and wine,
though no doubt consumed by swine.

Soul: To redeem the first illicit meal
we must eat again what we kill;
to grow purity in the impure
the rose is planted in manure.

SONNET OF A PHILO-SEMITE

The apotropaic onus now upon us
Is time-travel through a worm hole:
Depressing, puzzling, and perilous,
Like ratting on yourself as a mole.
To be and not to be;
Stopping (church) father from mating mother;
Hearing the gospels as calamity;
Seeing the Pharisee as brother.
Reading New Testament back to front,
Like the rabbis write Hebrew;
To reveal the reasons if not the moment
Jesus ceased to be a Jew.
    Our mirror must become our prism,
    Shining a light on Christian anti-Semitism.

A PRAYER TO AND FOR THE JEWISH PEOPLE, AFTER AUSCHWITZ

Mordecai won't bow down
To any but the Lord
So Shoah's *Schadenfreuden*
Brought night upon the world

Chosen by Life for life
Forsaken by the dead to death
G-d's last midwife
Faith's first breath

Gospels like loaded handguns
Left where small children play
Are complicit in the pogroms
Can't be explained away

Are Aryan genes selected?
No, it is untrue
Only the Gentiles elected?
No, Jesus was a Jew

Sinai to Calvary
Your sons scale heights
Sarah to Mary
Your daughters bear lights

Star of David
Fire menorah and cross
Infinite profit
Intimate loss

Praise divine goodness
Grant eternal peace
Teach us forgiveness
Forgive as we preach

Show us steadfast love
You suffer for our sins
Build a nest for the dove
You're where Shalom begins

Fallible and mortal
Dust like all the rest
Yet our truest portal
To a vision of the blest

Prophets of higher justice
Priests of holy law
Three cheers for the Jews
Torah, Torah, Torah!

POGROM'S PROGRESS: A CHRISTMAS POEM 2023

Eyes through the Season seeing
the light unto the nations
threatened with nonbeing
beset by abominations.

Jackals hunting on hind legs
lambs roasted on a spit
a mother murdered as she begs
and her husband's throat is slit.

Conscience a shadow of itself
Christmas a shadow of a shadow
humanity reduced to a feckless elf
prancing like old Jim Crow.

From the blasphemies of Hamas
must bleed the good out of evil
Jews and Christians on the cross
redeeming anti-Semitism primeval.

THE DESCENT OF GOODNESS

Goodness comes to those who wait
And court her like a Greek maiden
Who rebuffs utility as rape
Pleasure as pedestrian
Longing for an ecstatic union
Beyond happiness
Where kisses speak
Caresses feel
Limbs walk on water
Blessing silence with the gift of naming
Lighting the way to joy
For so many in the dark.

Body and soul rise to meet her
Only because she descends
An unknown goddess
From heights hidden underground
Depths plumbed into the sky
Wednesday's volcanic ash
That chastens rather than chokes
Heraclitus' flowing lava
That ignites but does not consume
Lifting new land as a benediction
Amid the sinking sea
Life in the tide of death.

It hurts to be so beautifully loved
We long for permanent possession
She immediately dispossesses
She knocks politely at the door
We resent the intrusion
Her lineage is uncertain
Rumored to be suspect
Her father Mars, mother Venus
Her earthly children fanatics
Who behead infidels like dolls
But genetic testing reveals
She is evolution itself.

MAKING SENSE OF CHRIST

When the world was without eyes,
You were the beauty of starlight.

When the world was without ears,
You were the cry of the newborn.

When the world was without hands,
You were the skill of the carpenter.

When the world was without news,
You were the gospel of the Jews.

When the world was without a tongue,
You were the word of truth.

When the world was without a heart,
You were incarnate love.

Make of me a new world of sense,
Able to see, hear, feel, smell, speak, and care.

CASTE AND CHRIST

The story of caste is stochastic:
blind luck decrees who is blind
for a time, who is sighted,
who is healthy, who blighted,
who is rich, who a beggar,
whether you are called "nigger."

The method of Christ is mechanical:
good gifts given for good
like a folio in a psalter,
a triptych on an altar,
eclipsing all pretension
by unfolding self-extension.

Eternal life is no fear of death,
hysteria of human history,
knowing nothing can be taken,
no one ever be forsaken,
by perfect singular Beauty
beyond both chance and duty.

ETERNAL RETURNS (12-25-2019)

Saint praying for sinner is
sinner without fail;
sinner prays for himself so
serpent swallows tail.

Virtues ground the body,
senses lift the soul;
heart of every diamond,
once a lump of coal.

Immaculate Sufficiency
made dust His common cause,
laughing us into being
giving eternity pause.

Can even silence say
if kenosis or insanity
drains the rancid humor
from crucified humanity?

So far fertile His 'hesed
this sterile winter morn
He aborts His only Son
so we may yet be born.

ONE SMALL STEP FOR MAN

Trinita dei Monti, atop the Spanish Steps,
Is closed for renovation;
Below, tourists take thirsty sips
From the Baraccia Fountain.

Tarps imprinted with the church façade
Keep pilgrims out but anticipating;
Above, rain clouds are a fusillade
Of holy water in waiting.

Would the restored sacristy itself,
Regilded a heavenly yellow,
Be still a book on a shelf,
A mirror in a bordello?

Do graduated icons of the mind
Point to transcendent love?
Can we not be happy or kind
With the inner psychic dove?

On Penrose's staircase impossible,
We meet ourselves coming and going;
The rendezvous is brief and risible,
An endless flight of unknowing.

Roman faith cleaves to the *Scala Sancta*,
Pilate's stairs to Christ's refulgence;

Retrieved from Jerusalem by Saint Helena,
They offer a plenary indulgence

To those who mount upon their knees,
Praying silently as they ascend
To the darkened Holy of Holies,
Blessing those who will attend.

Martin Luther made it half way up,
Then walked upright back down;
He decided to pass on suffering's cup
And to stomp the papal crown.

Half the West saw a giant leap,
The other a dwarfing fall;
Do works virtue's harvest reap
Or resistless grace do it all?

Regardless Johannes Climacus
Pines to scale highest paradise,
Inspiring you, me, and us
As we shuffle through this life.

STARING IT DOWN

Don't think it isn't suicide
that lights the way to God
for those denied a tender word
they might easily have heard
from our kindless lips.

Hidden in the neighbor's soul
is the church part and whole
for which hands could uphold
the fears and griefs left untold
to our self-waxed ears.

May love melt this frozen flesh
like lava boils the ocean depths
and dimmest moon eclipses sun
like the barrel of a gun
stared down by open eyes.

DEATH'S CAROLS[1]

Do not see the scenic birth of Christ
but the ugly death of Jesus
before we sold him into deity
for thirty pieces of silver screen,
Hollywood and our peace of mind,
back when he was a peasant son
working with his Father's wood,
calling Him only good.

Do not touch the clean hands of Pilate
but the dirty laundry of Caesar:
mortal Octavian turning divine Augustus
with his sanguine sword and simony,
and gloomy Tiberius purging treason
from the imperial Peace of Rome,
strangling Sejanus, starving Livilla,
crucifying the prophet of Judea.

Do not hear the blood curse of the Jews
but holocaust howls caused by Gentiles –
Americans, Germans, Russians, Iranians –
crossing the unwanted off the rolls
of manifest destiny, blood and honor,
classless society, final testament,
the way a bull swats a fly with its tail
and male enslaves female.

1. The phrase, "death's carols," is taken from Walt Whitman's "Out of the cradle endlessly rocking."

Do not taste the seasoned heroes of antiquity
but the sour anti-heroes of modernity.
Waters roll down to meet as equals,
reflecting justice, as Sweet Auburn's King
rests slain but free in his white marble crypt.
Yet un-freedom fills the square where alms
are illegal, and the Chapel of All Faiths
reeks of urine and is attended by wraiths.

Do not smell sweet memory of the past
but rank odor of present embodied sweat
rewarding strenuous effort with self-disgust
and anxious indulgence with more shame
that we may confess what elements are us.
Then will Jesus be resurrected at last
and those reach the height of love he lives
who consent to take even as he gives.

PEACE BY THE BOOK

Until Muslims become Christians,
Pierced ecstasy of Teresa,
Body's permanent visa
To all holy lands,
There will be no peace.

Until Christians become Jews,
Fluid justice of Amos,
Power purged of hubris
And the orphan's good news,
There will be no peace.

Until Jews become Muslims,
Sacred vertigo of Rumi,
Soul's only cure for calumny
And stolen diadems,
There will be no peace.

The Good Book reads best,
Writing the Abrahamic God
In hearts as bricks from one hod
Building sanctuaries East and West,
Where there can be peace.

A MODERN ODE

Unless You write in red dust
a destiny after death,
there is no You for us,
and courage loses breath.

Pindar says become the man you are,
find wisdom in wealth and repute,
but Plato raises virtue's bar
and commands the poets mute.

Whether deep or merely absurd,
being in time or eternity,
You spoke a most uncanny word
when you uttered me.

LARGILLIÈRE'S "ELIZABETH THROCKMORTON"

Her face floats over a billowing white habit
The sun breaking through cumulus clouds
Her lips two symmetrical red flares
Lighting the air with incandescent smile
Her modest yet manifold bosom
The swelling tide of the sea
That beckons you
Blesses you
But permits no entry
Lest you drown
In the breathless spirit it incarnates.

A black veil etches a heart on her forehead
Pointing to sainted eyes that paint you
As God sees you always
Unflinching yet forgiving
With the insouciance of goodness.

Her prayer of a right hand holds a book
The index finger holding a place
In interrupted time and space
I mumble the wedding vow
She whispers "I will change your life."

Nicolas de Largillière's "Elizabeth Throckmorton" (1729),
in the National Gallery of Art in Washington, D.C.

FOR SAINT ELIZABETH OF RUSSIA

The most beautiful woman in Europe
marries a noble yet timid aesthete;
the royal families of Russia hope
no hemophilic bloodlines to repeat;
the princess converts to the prince's creed,
but before she conceives daughter or son,
he's felled by revolutionary bombs;
she forgives his killers, for those in need
she surrenders her name and old fortune
to found a convent in new catacombs.

In an abandoned mine outside Moscow
the purest metal is cast by the crowd;
the dearest Romanov jewel like snow
melts equally for the meek and the proud;
annealed by service and the ego's noose,
her soul is bathed like ancient martyrs' robes
in the lambkin's blood running white not red;
she turns future Gulag prisoners loose
by removing Fabergé from her lobes
and placing thorns upon her willing head.

Elizabeth Feodorovna (1864-1918), Orthodox Nun
and Saint after being Grand Duchess of Russia

"FOLLOWING STEADFAST LOVE"

(Prayer to be sung w/ "The Pachelbel Canon in D," as performed by the Jean-François Paillard Chamber Orchestra)

[Introduction: bass and pizzicato violin, 8 beats unvoiced]

Dear God, [starts at 0:17]

My God,

Help me

Help you.

Your truth,

My mind;

Your good,

My will;

Your grace,

My hand;

Your life,

My death.

I will always follow you [1:03]

Because you always follow m-e

With your knowing truth . . . one truth, eternal;

I will follow you because you always follow m-e

With your willing good, dear God . . . perfect good, majestic;

I will follow you because you always follow m-e

With your touching grace, my God . . . cruciform grace, redemptive;

I will follow you because you always follow me.

Vital life, slain death, [2:04]

Help me, help you.

[String Interlude, unvoiced for a full minute] [2:19]

You follow, I follow . . . [with pizzicato strings, sotto vɔce] [3:19]

I follow, you follow . . .

You follow, so closely . . .

I follow, distantly . . .

You follow me, eternally . . . [sotto voce]   [3:33]

You follow me, majestic'ly . . .

You follow me, redemptively . . .

You follow me, with suffering . . .

I follow you, but fitfully . . .

I follow you, but timidly . . .

I follow you, but guiltily . . .

I follow you, in safety . . .

I would follow, when you follow . . . [increasingly forte]   [4:02]

I would follow, where you follow . . .

I would follow, how you follow . . .

I would follow, for you follow . . .

Me

MEN

With your steadfast love, with your steadfast love . . .   [4:17]

With your steadfast love, with your steadfast love . . .

With your steadfast love, with your steadfast love . . .

With your steadfast love, with your steadfast love . . .

WOMEN

With a sacred heart, with a sacred heart . . .   [4:32]

With a sacred heart, with a sacred heart . . .

With a sacred heart, with a sacred heart . . .

With a sacred heart, with a sacred heart . . .

MEN

With your knowing truth, you conceived of me . . .   [4:47]

With your willing good, you then let me be . . .

With your touching grace, you have felt the tree . . .

With the gift of life, you would set me free . . .

WOMEN

With the gift of life, overcoming world . . .   [5:02]

With the gift of life, overcoming self . . .

With the gift of life, overcoming death . . .

With a sense of sin, you humble me.

MIXED CHORUS

I'll always follow you   [5:18]

For you follow m-e

With a constant faith,

Dear God;

I'll always follow you

For you follow

With a blessed hope, with the surest hope;

My God,

I'll always follow you

For you follow

With incarnate love, with the purest love;

Our God,

We'll always follow you

For you follow,

Incarnating love

In u-s.

Oh Our Father, Lord and Father, [6:16]

Pl-ease take u-s;

Tender Son, Word and Son,

Pl-ease take u-s;

Holy Spirit, Breath and Spirit,

Please take us

Into your steadfast love.

IS THERE NONE GOOD?

Is life a fiction we write then die
not true or false, testament or lie
but thread by which we hang the sky?

Cliques and clowns end in dust
do and don't what they must
while priests imagine the just.

Gnostic daemons get the joke
the cosmic egg has no yolk
we are words a deaf-mute spoke.

So compose your heart and head
with viral metaphors you've read
but take no one to your bed.

For social distancing is key
to preserving you from me
both antimind and antibody.

Or does the Unseen beck us home
not to the Holy See of Rome
nor the U.S. Capitol dome?

But to the child who fell to earth
aborting Caesar by his birth
in the midst of our common filth.

Eudaimonism no altruist makes
evolution gives but what it takes
as the gene its own host forsakes.

No sanguine hero with tragic flaw
could dictate the forgiving law
by which a hand supplants a claw.

Teach louts and lovers to believe
each soul was meant to receive
a grace that knows how to grieve.

Then let the Good's will be done
feeding all, forgetting none
blessing the many in the One.

DIVINE TRIFECTA

Eros, agape, philia,
divine trifecta; yet historic Hialeah
lost its permit from the sunshine state
to teach its gamblers how to wait
for thoroughbreds to show their faces;
now they watch as remote races
are lost with chips at a casino
where flamingos go
for the fall.

May smiles and frowns
spring from Churchill Downs,
tracking forever Derby hats,
cigars, roses, Bourbon vats,
Ali's memory, Foster's songs,
as three-year-olds over ten furlongs
jockey our loves into focus,
seeing the homestretch in a fetus,
evening the odds for us all.

CODA: UNRULY DISCIPLINES

Physics would bind large and small,
cause and effect, in one coherent thought
but always comes to naught.

Poetry would wed innocence and experience,
beauty and truth, in one majestic verse
but only makes things worse.

Theology would unite the many loves
that time wears and eternity veils
but inevitably fails.

All our unruly disciplines declare
the Transcendent must tell its own story,
which we can only live as allegory.

Cross-eyed Guercino
bring into focus
with blessed strabismus
my erotic ego
and agapic God.

These poems, God's prayers to me,
came with silence all could see
distaste that drew feeling near
vision everyone could hear:
a black Lab asked me about death,
and my soul took its first breath.

LUX ET VERITAS?

> In Your light we see light.
>
> (PSALM 36:9)

turn this over in your mind
can consciousness ever find
itself
in an endless waving ocean
of blind matter in fixed motion?

can we vivisect our brains
and think everything remains
itself
after fact is amputated from wish
and soul grown in a petri dish?

Luther's *simul justus et peccator*
was the self's reformation *for*
itself
as paradoxical to Catholics
as quantum theory to physics.

finite light that should reveal reality
is but an absurd duality
itself
with Plato's sun trapped in the cave
at once a particle and a wave.

we who have missed the mark
must learn to see what the dark
itself
shows to reason and to faith
we spin the truth upon a lathe.

yet the crux of life and death
may be what gives us breath
itself
transubstantiated by eternal Love
collapsing freely from above.

THE AUSCHWITZ CROSS

The Polish evening pays no mind
to scions of Luther as they dine
on unleavened bread, kosher wine,
flesh and blood of ancient Palestine.

Is this not the Christian way
from Saint John down to today
to ask our guilt be washed away
by innocent Jews on whom we prey?

Our Father, may you be on earth
to give your kingdom second birth,
hallowing even crematorium oven,
the new cross for our old sin.

SHARING THE CROSS

The Holy God to bear alone
is harder than when two are one,
sharing with a single mind
the eternal challenge be kind,
knowing fraud and failure come
whether we speak or stay dumb.

Silence that is heard by two
is monotheism to the Jew;
when the Buddha transcended time,
he still asked the world to rhyme;
your suffering felt by me
adds us to the Trinity.

Words hold no higher glory
than to tell the common story
of how each life turns the page
of itself and the age,
as we are born and die
asking each other how and why.

FOR BLESSED BERNHARD LICHTENBERG, RIGHTEOUS AMONG THE NATIONS

Utter darkness usually begins
    with partial shadow,
as when a single bulb in the attic
    is extinguished
to pare the utility bill.

The stairway to stored memories
    is dimmed,
and no one cares to make the ascent
    anymore
to find the old diploma or wedding license.

The wolves of winter came down from the Alps
    to feed on spare ribs of children,
as the Vikings once gathered in Odin's Woods
    for the holy blót feasts.

Thought to be extinct in Austria and Italy
    but kept alive by hunger,
Canus lupis made a stunning comeback
    like Thor's uru hammer.

A Catholic light in the German mountain
    shone on the predators and prey:
"Outside burns the temple.
    This is also a place of worship."

But betrayed by two of Adam's ribs
    hearing him pray for the sheep,
the illumination was put out
    like a gauged eye.

So the stoked furnaces of Dachau
    cast their pagan penumbra,
reverting Bartimaeus and us
    to a beggared blindness.

RECONNOITERING FEMININITY

> [8] *Then he sent out the dove from him, to see if the waters had subsided from the face of the ground;* [9] *but the dove found no place to set its foot, and it returned to him to the ark, for the waters were still on the face of the whole earth. So he put out his hand and took it and brought it into the ark with him.* [10] *He waited another seven days, and again he sent out the dove from the ark;* [11] *and the dove came back to him in the evening, and there in its beak was a freshly plucked olive leaf; so Noah knew that the waters had subsided from the earth.* [12] *Then he waited another seven days, and sent out the dove; and it did not return to him any more.*
>
> (GENESIS 8:8–12)

Ovulating like Noah sending out a dove,
She asks if the flood waters have receded
and the scoured land is ready for life.

Will the dove return with an olive branch,
will yin meet yang and venture out of the ark
to start again cycles of breathing and drowning?

All were once sailors bobbing on the tide
of moons moving us thru the middle passage
between fallopian tube and uterus.

Nazi doctors studied the effects of stress,
including a certain death sentence,
on the reproductive systems of young women.

After being guillotined, corpses were analyzed:
did the anxiety of imminent beheading
affect their estrogen or progesterone levels?

We now live off romance on Chatterton Court,
as autonomy the arsenic of Femininity
waits for a child to abort.

To secure the sentence of death on death
we must love the serendipity of Woman's life,
the necessary condition of our own.

JUNE 24, 2022: THE HEALING DIET OF WORMS

To eat of eternity is to hunger for time
to regurgitate God to young chicks
chirping for warmth and worms.

We are all *terra animata*,
fledglings trying to sprout wings
before winter freezes earthen us.

Let love grow the weak to health
unthreatened by the dilation of death
and the curettage of hawks and coyotes.

We must sing out our mortal sins
not visiting them on the next generation
but grateful for the Golden Rule of life.

May the fifty-year ethical schism end
with reformation of our democratic nest
to include at last the demos as fetus.

If God loved us before we were,
this should be our task and spur:
fast from the diet of abortion,
feed every life its due portion.

GOD ALONE

Impossible effort must still be made
to believe in Love without afterlife,
even as Christ took to wife
the true church that never was.

God alone should be quite enough,
says the gate to Gethsemani;
there is time for eternity
in every fragile hourglass.

Immortality is vain,
insulting gracious Yahweh,
insisting He pre-pay
our final boarding pass.

If we awake from dreams of death
a resurrected company,
let it be serendipity
not the perk of a higher class.

Lest we put out the eye of pain
with the glamor of this fey world,
while those starving and cold
are abandoned en Mass.

The gated entrance to the Abbey of Gethsemani in Trappist, Kentucky

APOLOGIES TO PLATO

The living are born by recalling past life
Is but half of Plato's paradoxical equation;
The dead are slain by forgiving past strife.

With or without cross, drum, or fife,
Church and state assume cooperation;
The living are born by recalling past life.

Too long has husband lifted a hand to wife,
And though rape and rapists abomination,
The dead are slain by forgiving past strife.

With saints and martyrs now just as rife
As when spirit first blessed creation,
The living are born by recalling past life.

Too long has scripture made Jesus a knife,
Threatening the circumcised with castration;
The dead are slain by forgiving past strife.

After Socrates, we need no erotic midwife
To deliver the soul to eternal celebration.
The living are born by recalling past life.
The dead are slain by forgiving past strife.

SCALING MAN

Forgiveness is a gift of time,
grace allowing the self to rhyme
wandering foot and wounding line.
But who can give it?

Courage is a lack of chills
poised before a world that kills
alike buffalo and Bills.
But who can live it?

Justice is the ancient right
of the darkness and the light
never to hide in pained sight.
But who can see it?

Prudence is the master switch
not thrown by our inner bitch
to keep from being hit by pitch.
But who can free it?

Love is the eternal word
evolution calls absurd
yet all living things have heard.
But who can believe it?

Virtue is the scale of man,
whether a critic or fan.

Without question, each one can nevertheless receive it.

THE ORIGINAL SIN 2

The original sin was the first pratfall,
ourselves the butt of creation;
the bottomless serpent guffawed
at our claim to make information
received in an early trunk call
from distant station to station.
Boast you invent time and space,
then they come as pi in the face.

Portable radio tuned to a symphony,
wired for music already written,
to want more creative autonomy
is itself to be snake-bitten.
The Mega-Meta-Marconi
who put four fingers in the mitten
still left the thumb opposable
so we could dial in winter trouble.

DNA is a specified code found,
not fabricated, even as I find
my consciousness already bound
to a given body and taken mind.
Growth from an acorn in the ground
is not by majestic oak designed,
but a gift from the Being
of our uncanny becoming.

CHANNELING CATHERINE

Channeling Catherine of Siena,
I knee-beg the saint's *patientia*
for the descent into self
beyond happiness and wealth
to arise all egoless
paradox of fallen goodness.

But rude epiphany pain
plants itself within the brain;
like Knowledge in Eden's heart,
the tree that fells pious art
leaves me without saving face
unless her smile prove my grace.

THE GUT OF ROME

Shall we affirm the freedom of the will
Without the necessity of sainthood?
After the lung has supplanted the gill,
The creature must still consent to the good.
To deny oneself today is morbid,
To let the soul forage only healthy.
Poverty and chastity we forbid,
Making our protestant pockets wealthy.
Faith without works is the death of striving,
As the Epistle of James so well knew.
Thus the Gospel of once graceful living
Evaporates like the early morning dew.
Preaching irresistible election
Casts God the enemy of perfection.

INCARNATION

With sin, my body became my soul,
binding me to matter and to force;
by grace, God became my body,
freeing my soul from fallenness;
in Christ, human psyche and soma
are cobbled together on the cross,
so the whole person becomes a prayer.

To reverse evil is to live;
to dispel death is to have hated
(then forgiven) incarnation.

TRANSUBSTANTIATION

The atom split
when we tried to harness it
to our aggression.

        The Messiah left
        when he felt the wooden heft
        of our self-possession.

                The Reformation found its crucifix
                in the liberating remix
                of our Renaissance delusion.

                We must be opened to the energy
                of divine *agape*'s synergy,
                our fission into fusion.

        Thus will return the first cause
        that is ours and never was,
        the once and future science.

Or no forgiveness in sight
will be our final deathright,
the post-post-modern romance.

IN ADAM'S PLACE
(AFTER READING CATHERINE OF SIENA)

She who lives humility
speaks the Word that sets her free
from every judgment of sin
by herself or any men
with sublimest mercy's grace.

Compassion is never blind
voiding justice to be kind
but seeing with faith's pupil
upholds divine love's scruple
suffering in Adam's place.

THE THIRD EXCELLENCE
(AFTER READING JOHN OF THE CROSS)

What would it mean
to be able to give
more than we have
to one who needs nothing?

Can we who want everything
receive ourselves as given
with quiet the receipt
from Being to nonbeing?

Is or shall all be well
not because we love
or because we are loved
but because Love is itself?

AGAINST PERSONOLATRY: MY PRAYER OF SAINT SANDRA SABATTINI

Draw my heart like the rein of a steed,
instrument of your will;
send me to extremity of need,
and I shall go farther still.

Seal my gaze to heal as holy
the sick in body and soul;
bind my will to kindness only
as You are kind to all.

Mortality mourned is immortality;
lament for the dead keeps time
in constant tune with eternity,
making past and present rhyme.

Every child carried to term is chastity;
to bear abortion of self for another
is autonomy bowing to sanctity,
our true father and mother.

To lose my mind for You is sanity;
remembering to forget and forgive
the impatience and the vanity
by which we personolaters live.

Blessed Sandra Sabattini (1961–1984)

FOR SAINTS WEIL AND HILLESUM

Many souls are stained by hate
of temporal evils they are not
eternity always comes too late
for selves we were then forgot.
The mind mined in *Mein Kampf*
is mine and yours and ours
inner Nazis douse love's lamp
and burn to ash the stars.
When Jesus is the son of Moses
embodied in the saints again
every horse will win the roses
and mad women shall be man.
    This truth won't be denied,
    genocide is suicide.

FINALE

How to read the Author of the Word,
touch the Mover of time,
make room for the Architect of space,
when I am the sight of darkness,
the feeling of frozen water,
a squatter who lost his place?

See the ram under a pall
of snow on stone in faith
now a signature on a receipt
from a company out of state
with an unlisted number
but files you can't delete.

"A dog may as well speculate
on the mind of Newton,"
said Darwin in tolerant despair.
Will an unknown goddess
put her ear to my soul
and listen to this prayer?

truth is my favorite lie
goodness is my pride
beauty but a Bourbon high
without her by my side.